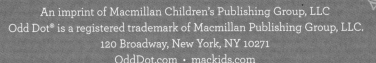

Joyful Books for Curious Minds

An imprint of Macmillan Children's Publishing Group, LLC

Odd Dot® is a registered trademark of Macmillan Publishing Group, LLC.

120 Broadway, New York, NY 10271

OddDot.com • mackids.com

EDITORS Nathalie Le Du and Kate Avino

DESIGNER Caitlyn Hunter

PRODUCTION EDITOR Mia Moran

PRODUCTION MANAGER Jocelyn O'Dowd

Library of Congress Control Number: 2024010817

ISBN 978-1-250-37193-5

Our books are available at special discounts when purchased in bulk for premiums and sales promotions as well as for fund-raising or educational use. Special editions or book excerpts also can be created to specification. For details, contact the Macmillan Corporate and Premium Sales Department at (800) 221-7945 ext. 5442, or send an email to MacmillanSpecialMarkets@macmillan.com.

This work is an independent biography and is not authorized, sponsored, or endorsed by Beyoncé.

First edition, 2024

Printed in the United States of America by Phoenix Color, Hagerstown, Maryland

1 3 5 7 9 10 8 6 4 2

A Book for the Littlest Beyoncé Fans

You Are Fierce

illustrated by Nneka Myers

New York

You are fierce, baby.

A gift that comes only
once in a lifetime.

A girl who wastes no time.

You dream . . .
of blazing like a star.

You're young, but you're ready.

No, no, no!
No one can
dim your light.

You shine . . .
falling deeper in
love with your dream,

working hard till you hold it.

Growing, learning . . .

. . . becoming our everything.

You create . . .
worlds of possibilities
all around,

a legacy rich with
    your own regal history,

a joyful future.

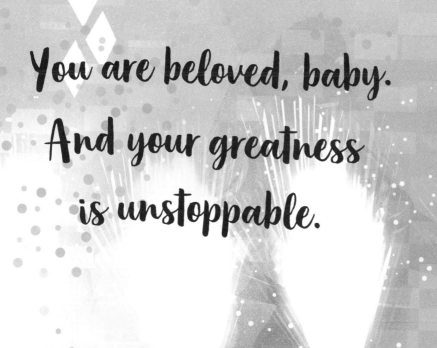

You are beloved, baby.
And your greatness
is unstoppable.